Listen To Your Instincts

MacGregor, Cynthia

Lex: 550   R.L.: 3.3   Pts: 2

THE ABDUCTION PREVENTION LIBRARY™

LISTEN TO YOUR INSTINCTS

Cynthia MacGregor

The Rosen Publishing Group's
PowerKids Press™
New York

Published in 1999 by The Rosen Publishing Group, Inc.
29 East 21st Street, New York, NY 10010

First Edition

Book Design: Danielle Primiceri

Photo Credits: Cover Donna M. Scholl; pp. 4, 7, 8, 11, 12, 13, 15, 16, 19, 20 © Seth Dinnerman.

MacGregor, Cynthia.
    Listen to your instincts/ by Cynthia MacGregor.
        p.   cm. — (The abduction prevention library)
    Includes index.
    ISBN 0-8239-5249-5
    1. Abduction—Prevention—Juvenile literature. 2. Kidnapping—Prevention—Juvenile literature.
    3. Children and strangers—Juvenile literature. 4. Safety education—Juvenile literature.
    5. Instinct—Juvenile literature. I. Title. II. Series.
    HV6571.M33 1998
    613.6—dc21   97-49227
                                                                                        CIP
                                                                                        AC

Manufactured in the United States of America

Contents

1 What Are Instincts? 5

2 Using Your Instincts 6

3 Mara 9

4 Instincts or Manners? 10

5 Trust Yourself First 13

6 "It Can Be Our Secret" 14

7 Obey Your Instincts 17

8 Making a Scene 18

9 Being Safe at Home 21

10 A Reminder 22

Glossary 23

Index 24

What Are Instincts?

Todd and Jamal were walking home from the park. They came to an old, empty building.

"Hey!" Todd said. "Let's explore that building. I want to see what's inside."

"I don't think that's a good idea," Jamal said. "It might be **dangerous** (DAYN-jer-us)."

"You're right," Todd said. "Let's go home."

Something inside Jamal told him not to go into the building. Jamal was listening to his **instincts** (IN-stinkts). Instincts are feelings inside of us that give us hints about what to do in certain **situations** (sit-choo-AY-shunz).

◀ *Your friends may say and do things that may not always be a good idea for you to do.*

Using Your Instincts

Most people are nice. But some people and some situations can be dangerous. A dangerous person may say things to try to **convince** (kun-VINS) you to go with him. But you have special tools to help you. You can think about the right thing to do. And you can listen to your instincts.

For example, you know you shouldn't go somewhere with a stranger or someone you don't know well. Sometimes it may look like fun. But listen to your instincts and say no.

A shortcut may seem like a good idea, but listen to your instincts. What are they telling you? ▶

Mara

A man stopped Mara near school. "I'm making a TV show," the man said. "Would you like to be on TV? Get in my car and I'll take you to where we're filming."

At first Mara thought, Wow! I can be on TV! But something about the man made Mara nervous. So Mara listened to her instincts. Mara didn't know this man. And a good person would want to ask Mara's parents about the TV show first.

Mara was smart. She said "No" and hurried away.

◀ *Your instincts can tell you if something is too good to be true.*

9

Instincts or Manners?

Larry was walking to his friend's house. He passed a woman who was standing by her car. "Where is the nearest gas station?" the woman asked.

"It's two blocks that way," Larry said.

"I'm having trouble with my car," the woman said. "And I'm all alone. Will you go with me to the gas station?"

Larry's mom had taught him to be helpful. But his instincts told him something was wrong. He didn't know this woman. Larry ran back to his house.

Don't worry about being impolite if your instincts tell ▶ you to get away. Your safety is most important.

Trust Yourself First

Bobby was home with a cold. Bobby's mom had to go to the store for some medicine.

"I'll be back in a few minutes," his mother said. "Don't open the door for anybody."

"Okay," Bobby said.

Soon after Bobby's mom left, someone knocked on the door. Bobby could see through the peephole that it was a woman. She looked very nice. But Bobby listened to his instincts and didn't open the door. When Bobby's mother got home, Bobby told her what had happened. Bobby's mom was proud of him.

◀ *Make a list of things that you should do to stay safe. Be sure to follow it when you're home alone.*

13

"It Can Be Our Secret"

You can usually trust people whom your parents say can be trusted. That could be people of **authority** (uh-THOR-ih-tee), such as your relatives, teachers, and police officers. But what if your instincts warn you about one of these people?

Suppose your teacher says, "Come to my house and we'll watch a movie. But don't tell anyone—it will be our secret." If something like this doesn't sound right, trust your instincts and say no. Also, you should tell your mom or dad about it right away.

It's important to tell your parent about anything that makes you uncomfortable. ▶

Obey Your Instincts

What if someone who you're supposed to **obey** (oh-BAY) tells you to do something that you think is wrong? Suppose a man says he's a police officer and shows you a badge. Then he says that you have to go in the car with him to meet your parents. Your instincts can tell you whether the man can be trusted. If your instincts tell you not to go with him, don't go. It may seem strange, but sometimes you have to obey your instincts before you obey someone of authority.

◀ *If obeying someone of authority, such as your dad's friend or a neighbor, makes you uncomfortable, listen to your instincts.*

Making a Scene

Your parents probably tell you, "Don't make a scene." But if someone scares you in a public place, you *should* make a scene. This means that if someone grabs your arm and says "Come with me," and you can't get away, you should yell as loud as you can. You can yell, "Don't take me away!" or "You're not my father!" or "You're not my mother!" This way people who are around you will understand what is happening. Your instincts tell you to yell when you're in trouble. Listen to them.

Making a scene may feel like a bad thing to do, but it can save you from getting into danger. ▶

Being Safe at Home

You know that you're safe at home. But trouble can sometimes happen at home, even on the computer. You can type messages to some nice people through the computer when you're **on-line** (on-LYN). But you can come across some bad people, too, just as you can outside of your home. On-line, an adult may pretend to be someone that he's not, such as a kid. This person isn't pretending for fun. He pretends because he is dangerous. He may even want to meet you. If any of these things happen, tell your mom or dad right away.

◄ *Be smart: Don't tell someone on-line what your name or phone number is.*

A Reminder

Your instincts are important. Sometimes they might be wrong, but more often they are right. There may be times when you get an **uncomfortable** (un-KUMF-ter-bul) feeling about someone or a certain situation makes you feel strange.

Your instincts may be wrong about the person or situation. But it's better to be careful. Listening to your instincts is the smart thing to do.

Glossary

authority (uh-THOR-ih-tee) Knowing a lot about something.

convince (kun-VINS) To make you believe something.

dangerous (DAYN-jer-us) Not safe; harmful.

instincts (IN-stinkts) The feelings each of us has inside of us that give us hints about what to do in a situation.

obey (oh-BAY) To do what you are told.

on-line (on-LYN) A world-wide computer system where a person can get information and communicate with others.

situation (sit-choo-AY-shun) A problem; an event that happens.

uncomfortable (un-KUMF-ter-bul) Feeling scared or unsure of something.

Index

A
authority, 14, 17

C
careful, 22
computer, 21
convince, 6

D
dangerous, 5, 6, 21

F
feelings, 5

N
nervous, 9

O
obey, 17
on-line, 21

P
parents, telling or asking, 9, 13, 14, 21
peephole, 13
police officer, 14, 17

S
saying no, 6, 9
scene, making a, 18
secrets, 14
situation, 5, 6, 22
stranger, 6

T
trust, 14, 17

U
uncomfortable, 22

W
warning, 14
wrong, 10, 17, 22

Y
yell, 18